Doing
Business
Globally

D1280733

The Lessons Learned Series

Wondering how the most accomplished leaders from around the globe have tackled their toughest challenges? Now you can find out—with Lessons Learned. Concise and engaging, each volume in this new series offers twelve to fourteen insightful essays by top leaders in business, the public sector, and academia on the most pressing issues they've faced.

A crucial resource for today's busy executive, Lessons Learned gives you instant access to the wisdom and expertise of the world's most talented leaders.

Other Books in the series:

Doing
Business
Globally

LES50NS
Boston, Massachusetts

Printed in the United States of America
12 11 10 09 08   5 4 3 2 1

Library of Congress Cataloging-in-Publication Data

Doing business globally.
    p. cm. — (Lessons learned)
ISBN 978-1-4221-2647-9 (pbk. : alk. paper)
1. International trade.
2. International business enterprises.
 HF1379.D65 2008
 658'.049—dc22

                        2008036458

In partnership with Fifty Lessons, a leading provider of digital media content, Harvard Business School Press is pleased to announce the launch of Lessons Learned, a new book series that showcases the trusted voices of the world's most experienced leaders. Through the power of personal storytelling, each book in this series presents the accumulated wisdom of some of the world's best-known experts, and offers insights into how these individuals think, approach new challenges, and use hard-won lessons from experience to shape their leadership philosophies. Organized thematically, according to the topics at the top of managers' agendas—leadership, change management, entrepreneurship, innovation, and strategy, to name a few—each book draws from Fifty Lesson's extensive video library of interviews with CEOs and other thought leaders.

A Note from the Publisher

Here, the world's leading senior executives, academics, and business thinkers speak directly and candidly about their triumphs and defeats. Taken together, these powerful stories offer the advice you'll need to take on tomorrow's challenges.

We invite you to join the conversation now. You'll find both new ways of looking at the world, and the tried-and-true advice you need to illuminate the path forward.

⊰ CONTENTS ⊱

Contents

Contents

Doing
Business
Globally

Local Versus Global

Maurice Lévy

Chairman and CEO, Publicis Groupe

GLOBALIZATION IS AN important subject. It is full of dangers and opportunities. If we look at the balance today, economically, globalization has brought a lot of richness to many countries and has helped a lot of countries improve the standard of living of their population.

At the same time, we are in danger of hurting people in their lives. For example, they are used to going to an outlet; then all of a sudden the name has changed because it has been bought. Or they were used to buying a product, and all of a sudden the company has been bought and they have the same product under a new brand, which is a global brand. This is leading to depersonalization. If we have a responsibility as people in communication, it is clearly to bring culture and life into this brand.

I will tell you a story, which goes back to the '70s. I was making a presentation, and I was very nervous. I was the young CEO of Publicis, and we had an extremely important international client, Colgate-Palmolive. We were showing a commercial for dishwasher soap, and it went very well. At the end of the commercial, there was a small kiss. It was not a French kiss, just a kiss.

The head of the communication department at that time, from New York, said, "Why do you need the kiss?"

I said, "We think it's charming."

He replied, "But it has nothing to do with the product."

Local Versus Global

I said, "Yes, but communication and advertising in France isn't hard selling. Hard selling is not something that works very well. We have our culture. It's difficult, as we have to engage people, and we have to create something that helps them understand that it's not only hard selling or hard commerce."

He jumped over his chair, knocked his head against the wall, and said, "This is unacceptable. Your differences are unacceptable. One day, you will eat hamburgers like we do; you will drink our soft drinks. You will become like us, and you will think like us!"

He was a very important client, so I was a little bit scared. I tried to explain, and I had some difficulty, so I took him to dinner. We had good wine, we had good food, and he ate very well.

I said, "So you see, you can drink good wine and you can eat very good food, but we don't ask you to think like us."

He laughed, and everything went well.

To connect with the people, brands have to carry values that are shared universally or values that carry something specific to the brand. For example, if you have a cosmetic and you are selling the beauty of Paris, it's fine; otherwise, a brand must always be rooted in something that is strong to the values of the people.

The challenge for us is how to make a global brand while at the same time being rooted in the culture of different countries. And that is not easy. One of the things you have to do is understand your target audience locally: what the brand means for the target audience, how they are using the product, and what is relevant to them.

If you do that, sometimes you will find things that are relevant in two or three countries, and you can use a campaign across for three, four, or more countries. At other times you have to develop a campaign that is very local.

You cannot only have a global view. When you have a global view, you are looking at the globe from such a height that you don't see anything, and you are just on the [surface] of the reality. You have to go deep down into countries and make your company and your brand relevant not only to your consumer but also to the population.

TAKEAWAYS

- ⚐ To connect with people, brands must carry universally shared values or values that carry something specific to the brand.

- ⚐ The challenge lies in creating a global brand while at the same time achieving relevance to the cultures of different countries.

- ⚐ A global view is not enough. You must dig down and make your brand relevant to both the consumer and the larger population.

———◆◆◆———

Integrating Global Business at a Local Level

———◆◆◆———

Neville Isdell

*Chairman, Board of Directors, and CEO,
The Coca-Cola Company*

AS YOU LOOK at globalization, you have
to look at it in two ways, because the era that
got the likes of Coca-Cola to being almost
a global company are different from the
requirements for a globalizing company to
be successful in the future. In the past, it

was about putting out your footprint alone. Now I think it's a little more than that.

The way that I like to look at it is this: in this world today, where globalization is being queried, where there is potential for the rise of economic nationalism, you have to be an integral and functioning part, both in perception and in reality, of every community in which you operate. Now, the franchise system's great, because it enables you to do that, because by and large, you are working with local companies and local entrepreneurs. You are localized.

I think that that connection back to the [culture] of each of those societies, in the right way, is where one has to be if one is going to continue to be a successfully globalizing company. The days of parachuting in and thinking that you bring superior knowledge and expertise into some of these countries is not necessarily true. You have to identify yourselves with the societies as a whole.

One of the areas that we have identified, which is very important to us, is water. Water is, obviously, integral to what we do. Now, how do people view our access to water? In some instances, where we haven't had what you might want to call social license, it's seen that when we are taking the water, extracting it, and not adding anything back that maybe our legitimacy can be queried. I don't believe that is a correct interpretation, but that is a reality, and I say it in terms of the perception that some people have. So what do you do?

There are areas in Kenya, for example, that are water-stressed. Do we have a major issue in Kenya? No. We have a major program providing water to schools, and we do this with other NGOs at the same time. We're also in certain water-stressed areas, looking after the watershed, to see that the aquifer is properly replenished. And, of course, we're also reducing our own footprint, our own usage of water, in terms of being sure that we're able to be as effective and efficient as possible. And while it doesn't always work perfectly, that really is what you have to do.

I've taken a specific [example] that is relevant to [Coca-Cola]. You need—always—to focus on something that is relevant to your business. Otherwise, you won't take it seriously. You won't do it well. And your people will not identify with it.

TAKEAWAYS

- ◻ What organizations did in the past to achieve global greatness is no longer applicable for companies that aspire to globalize successfully in the future.

- ◻ Companies today must be an integral and functioning part, both in perception and in reality, of every community in which they operate.

- ◻ Focusing on relevance to your own business and the local community is imperative. Otherwise, you won't take your commitment seriously.

———•••———

Understand the Differences When Doing Business Abroad

Andrew Sherman

Cofounder and CEO, Grow Fast Grow Right

———•••———

WE'RE LIVING IN a world particularly influenced by the Internet, where small companies are now able to do business abroad much more effectively. The Internet was the great leveler of the playing field in so many ways, in that [most] types of access barriers and communication barriers are gone as a result of our connectivity to each other. That's the good news.

The bad news is that we still are from different countries and speak different languages and do different kinds of things. Even [between] the United States and Canada, the United States and Australia, and the United States and the United Kingdom, there are major differences in the ways people do business.

Just last week I was hosting a group of female U.K. entrepreneurs, and we had a very intense three-hour session over the differences between their challenges as female entrepreneurs in the United Kingdom versus the United States. The differences were significant.

The story here is that all the companies that have been enabled and empowered to go abroad, because of the Internet and the great communication tools that we have, have lost sight of the fact that there are still major differences in culture, practice, customs, negotiation style, commerce, currency—in almost everything that you can think of.

And so what I'm really excited about is the access issue. What I'm concerned about is that we've all forgotten our differences. And if you forget the differences in going global, it's going to be a messy and embarrassing situation. Just because you *can* sell, via e-commerce, to a country eight thousand miles away doesn't mean that you *should* sell to a country eight thousand miles away if there are going to be problems in getting paid, if there are going to be problems in translation.

We've seen countless mistakes over the last couple of years: differences in packaging, pricing structure, and consumption; or differences in how to choose strategic marketing partners in those countries; or even overlooking the need for a strategic marketing partner in the first place. [You need] to understand that just because you're enabled on an e-commerce perspective doesn't substitute the need for some local representation, someone who's going to be out there.

If you say, "We've studied all the available markets, and for our product and service, Germany would be a really great market for us," first of all, you get an A in my book, because you've actually studied the market and figured this out. Some companies go into these things willy-nilly; they're pulled into marketplaces instead of [pushing themselves] into marketplaces. So they're getting a call from a prospective customer five thousand miles away, and they're so excited by the phone call that they start doing business in that country without really studying things.

But the point is: in smaller companies, the costs are higher. A larger company can get into a foreign marketplace, they can incur the overhead, they can hire people. Smaller companies make mistakes by going abroad. It can have a much greater impact on their profitability, operations, and infrastructure.

Understand the Differences

So go into these global markets, but go carefully. Go with the research, go with the right local market partners, understand differences in culture and differences in doing business, and just because we can talk to each other more easily, there's no substitute for getting on that airplane and meeting people and studying the culture and understanding really what doing global business is all about.

One great story that I enjoy sharing is that a few years ago I was in Taipei. I was speaking at the China Productivity Center and lecturing to a bunch of Taiwanese- and Pacific Rim—oriented businesses that wanted to come into the United States. And so we were talking about some of these lessons from doing business from the U.S. perspective.

I had been to three or four nights of restaurants in Taipei, and I was kind of hungry for some [American-style] food—food that I could recognize, food that I could pronounce. So they asked me on my last night

where I would like to go, and I answered,
"Pizza Hut." I don't mean this to be an
endorsement for Pizza Hut, but we went to
the Pizza Hut in downtown Taipei. What
I noticed on the menu was the same trade
dress, same waitress uniforms, same everything. The only difference between the
Pizza Hut in Taipei and the Pizza Hut that
you would get in the United States was the
toppings selection.

What I've often used as a story in teaching global business, international business is
think of your global business strategy like a
pizza. Okay? There are four elements of the
pizza: there's the crust, the cheese, the sauce,
and the toppings. Three of those things were
the same at all Pizza Huts across the world,
but the toppings varied by marketplace.

For every company, there's probably four
or five core components of their product
or service offering, and they really need to
maintain some consistency in those components as they go abroad. But don't forget
the toppings. Don't forget that in markets
adjustments will need to be made. If you
make your adjustments too big, you've lost

the integrity of your core product, but if you make no adjustments at all, you're forcing people to eat toppings that they really don't like or enjoy and aren't reflective of local culture.

I hate to boil down all teachings of global business strategy into pizza toppings, but in many ways that's what it's really all about.

TAKEAWAYS

- ⚔ Although the Internet has erased access and communication barriers, the fact remains that we still are from different countries, speak different languages, and have different cultures.

- ⚔ To succeed abroad, think of global business strategy like a pizza. Start with the crust, the cheese, and the sauce, and then vary your toppings by market.

Doing Business Globally

⚜ Realize that you will have to make market adjustments, but don't go so far that you lose integrity or remain so similar that the local culture doesn't respond.

Communicating Across Cultures

Sir David Bell

Director for People, Pearson

THE BIGGER AND more international
you are as a business, the more you have to
be thinking all the time: how are we going
to make people from very different cultures
understand that they're all part of the same
company? That is a real challenge.

Years ago, the American man who was
then running our education business came
to England to talk to some of his people.

They had done some work for him and he said to them, "I think that was really quite a good piece of work." Afterward, he said to me, "David, I told them I thought it was quite a good piece of work, and they all looked really depressed."

I said, "That, Larry, is because the word 'quite' means one thing in English-English and a different thing in American-English. In American-English, if you say 'quite good' it means 'very good.' In English-English, it normally means '[nice try].'"

His English people had taken away that he thought what they had done was very bad; what he actually meant was that it was very good. So you have to think when you communicate and when you deal with people from different backgrounds because the common understanding is less than you think it is.

How do we deal with that? There are a number of ways, and one of them is to begin to move people from one country to another and from one company to another. We have a big program to try and encourage people to work in another country or another company within Pearson, because when they do that they quickly begin to understand cultural differences. We bring all of our senior managers together once a year for three days, and gradually we've all come to understand each other really well. But it takes time.

The first time was a complete disaster. We had an English-style pantomime, and we'd just bought a big chunk of our education business, so we had twenty of our new American managers. We hired some people from an acting group to [stage] a murder mystery, which involved Marjorie Scardino [CEO of Pearson] being stabbed to death and various politically incorrect jokes. Our American colleagues couldn't understand this at all, and I tried to explain. I said, "Don't worry, the pantomime is an old English tradition where the leading man is played by a woman and the leading woman is played by a man." As I was saying this, I could see them thinking, "This proves it; these people are complete freaks."

Doing Business Globally

If you're buying a business where the language is completely different, you have to be three times as careful and you have to rely on the local management. You have to make sure that the person running it for you really understands English, or have people who really understand Japanese or Chinese. To really understand is not the same as nodding. Sometimes we find quite significant misunderstandings with some of our businesses for which English is not the first language.

We're trying to cultivate a set of values for the business, so that when you get five, ten, or twenty people from the company from different parts of the world together, they'll all value the same things.

TAKEAWAYS

- The more global your business, the more care you must take to get people from different cultures to realize they're part of the same organization.

- You must also take precautions and think when you communicate because common understanding is less than you think.

- To overcome cultural differences, rely on local management and bring together people from across the business so that the organization's overall values are consistent regardless of physical location.

International Business

Sir Bob Reid

Chairman, ICE Clear Europe

INTERNATIONAL BUSINESS IS extremely important when you ask yourself the question, "How do you adapt from one circumstance to another?" It's a simple thing. You must understand that people living in different parts of the world think differently and have different norms—and it's going to take you time to understand that.

Doing Business Globally

Moving from West Africa to Thailand is really quite different. The West Africans are the most ebullient, outgoing, gregarious, noisy, and rambunctious people, and they don't expect you to agree with them. They look for a contention, so that they can argue something through. And in the course of that argument, they grow to like you. Then you thrash out what you're going to do, and then you find out why you've done it wrong. And you laugh, and you start again.

When you go to a place like Thailand, [people] expect you to listen and understand their position. They expect you to make an input, but as an input that is conditioned—as it may be relevant or not relevant—and made in a much softer fashion in a much lower key and, in fact, done perhaps over a space of meetings. There's no need for speed; you take time. Nothing happens quickly. You make sure, whereas the Nigerians want it to happen tomorrow.

In the 1960s two of my Nigerian friends went to see [some people] in Japan, and they expected to go in, tell them what they want to do, and say, "This is what we want you to agree to." And the Japanese had never seen these people before. They didn't know who they were, and they had absolutely no understanding, so they achieved nothing.

They came back very disappointed and said, "We don't understand these people."

I said, "That's not the point. They don't understand you. That's much more important. They don't understand what you're after."

We all have that when we go from one society to another, and we must take care to understand. In some cases, it can be much quicker than others, and you must understand, learn, adjust, and adapt. You can't import your own philosophies and your own processes into a situation in which these could well be found to be alien.

The first thing to do is to listen and watch, and then decide how much of your past experience and the way in which you do things is actually going to work in that new situation. What would work in Nigeria might well not work in Thailand. What would work in Australia might well not work in England. And in all these situations, it's not a racial thing; it's a situational thing. Therefore, you must take time to understand what you are in, what the norms of that situation are, and then you make your adaptability after you've listened and learned for some time.

TAKEAWAYS

- ⇥ People in different parts of the world think differently and have different norms. Understanding these differences from a business perspective is vital.

- ⇥ Instead of approaching business as "We don't understand these people," approach it as "They don't understand you."

🔆 Don't assume that works in one country or situation will work similarly in another. Take the time to listen, watch, and truly understand.

Behavior Is the Language of International Business

Bryan Sanderson

Former Chairman, Standard Chartered

MAKE SURE THAT you reflect the places in which you operate in all that you do; that there is an openness to all sorts of ethnic and other forms of diversity, and a listening and open culture. And, in parallel,

Doing Business Globally

[recognize] that there is a common culture within the organization that people
understand, can relate to, and can express
themselves in.

At the end of the day, there has to be
crisp and clear communication; and that
can only be [achieved] through a common
language—both in the specific sense of the
word (English in our case) and also in the
broader sense of having common ethics,
guidelines, and principles that everybody
subscribes to and buys into.

A long time ago, before English was quite
as common as it is now, I used to go to Japan to sell crude oil. That was in about the
mid-1970s. It worked very well, as long as
the rules of courtesy were maintained.

Japanese courtesies are very important,
very long-winded, and take a long time.
However, they are absolutely vital; because
what effectively is happening—and I've since
had a lot of Asian experience and it happens
to a lesser or greater degree in other countries around Asia—is that the courtesies and
development of a personal relationship over

Behavior Is the Language

a period of time are a substitute for lots of
other things that would apply elsewhere.
They are almost a substitute for corporate
law, because corporate law is not nearly as
important or well understood there as it is
in an Anglo-Saxon country.

People put much greater store on a
handshake, on friendship, and on the word
of an individual with whom they are deal-
ing, rather than looking at the detailed
wording of a contract or where the semi-
colon is—which a British or American lawyer
will delightfully rip into and take on in
contractual law.

The way we behave is not understood
in most Asian countries. They think that
is thoroughly dishonest. What they believe
to be important is the spirit of the agree-
ment and your personal relationship; you
personally are accountable for what you said
and for what the understanding was. That
sort of understanding and relationship can
only be reached through good behavior, and
through behavior inside some boundaries of
courtesy that are internationally recognized.

Doing Business Globally

You need a corporate culture that is open and sympathetic, and ultra-tolerant of different cultures and diversity in all its forms—gender, ethnicity, sexual proclivity, disability, the whole lot. It has to be thoroughly open, and that has to be absolutely cemented into the company and the line management to the point where nobody even thinks about it.

There must also be a common culture, because there must be a common language in any company. At Standard Chartered Bank we do inculcate that. We do it through a host of formal training programs and a lot of work and effort.

In essence, banks are about the people within them. They don't have much hard capital. It really is a people business from start to finish, and our employees have to be responsible to the customers, so we have to make sure that they reflect the customers' social mores within the place we work. And, on top of that, we have to set standards that are admired.

Behavior Is the Language

We spend a lot of time at the Bank on good practice and on the softer issues of being a company. This becomes increasingly important as the company grows in size and complexity, particularly as it starts to cross national boundaries and contain within its compass lots of different cultures and perhaps ethnic groups. So increasing diversity means, in my view, that there should be much more attention on behavior.

TAKEAWAYS

- Wherever you operate and in all that you do, support an openness to ethnic and other forms of diversity.

- Cultivating such a culture is even more important as the organization grows in size, complexity, and location.

Doing Business Globally

✠ Because behaviors vary culturally and are often misunderstood, cultivating an ultra-tolerant culture within your own organization is critical.

———◆———

Prepare Thoroughly and Know Your Audience

Rosabeth Moss Kanter

Professor of Business Administration,
Harvard Business School

———◆———

AFTER THE SUCCESS of my book *World Class*, I had been doing a great deal of management consulting in Asia. I was well known and recognized as a good speaker, so

Doing Business Globally

I had opportunities to speak at very important platforms on very important programs.

I was particularly pleased to have an invitation to address a group of Asian CEOs in Bangkok, Thailand. I looked at the program and thought, "I have a wonderful position. The opening speaker [is] going to be the prime minister of Malaysia. Isn't that wonderful? I follow a prime minister. That's quite a compliment."

I prepared my usual material. I was told to talk about global competitiveness and the things that make companies world-class. I was ready.

I listened to the prime minister's speech. As he talked, he became more and more inflammatory and anti-Western. That was the time when he was scoring political points by contrasting so-called Asian values with so-called Western values. I simply didn't realize the effect he was having on the audience.

When I got up to speak, I didn't quite get that I had several strikes against me. Yes, I was female, but I did have my credentials.

Prepare Thoroughly

But I was also American, and I hadn't quite
realized what a handicap that was going
to be. Since most of my experiences and
stories were American, I tried to deflect it
as I began with a joke about how they were
experts on Asia and I was an expert on
American companies. But nobody laughed,
and I should have understood then. It was
the worst speech of my life. I have never
been not well received and I was very rattled
and concerned about it.

I learned some lessons that now drive
everything I do: you'd better know your
audience, who else is speaking, and the
context. If you don't know the context and
you just go into a meeting prepared to do
your own thing, you can fail—even if your
own thing is very, very good and usually
well received.

I had not spent enough time thinking
about the context. Well, believe me, now I
do. I'm relentless about preparation, about
thinking through who's in the audience. I
want to know who they are and what their

views are. I want to know who else is speaking and what the goal of the meeting is. I mean thorough preparation.

I was always a very prepared person—I don't want to make it sound like I'm casual—but today I look more at the context. That speech was nearly ten years ago and I now collect more information and work on being very prepared.

Also, you can't take success for granted. I had done extremely well and I assumed I would continue to do well. That kind of confidence is important, but you can't take it for granted. Every occasion and event is a new game. You have to be prepared to play that particular game and not coast on past successes.

In everyday work situations, the important lesson is about the value of preparation and asking questions: Who is the audience for this memo? Who will be at the meeting? Who will care about the results of the meeting? What do they value and stand for? What do they want to hear from you? The more you think about the audience, the point, and the purpose, the more successful you will be.

Then, overprepare—not that it's so rehearsed that you can't be flexible and spontaneous but so that you're prepared for any contingency. I wasn't. I had to try to finesse this on the spot. I hadn't thought about what would happen if somebody didn't like my message.

Because communication skills are the essence of what today's managers do—they are always presenting themselves in front of employees, colleagues, upper management, and customers—they really have to understand preparation and audience.

TAKEAWAYS

⚔ Before making a presentation, especially to a global audience, take the time to prepare. Know your audience,

Doing Business Globally

know who else is speaking, and be sure that you understand the context.

❧ Not knowing the context can cause a normally successful presentation to fail. Never take past successes for granted.

❧ Whether you're presenting to you staff or to new customers on the other side of the globe, always prepare thoroughly and plan for contingencies.

International Companies Should Have International Boards

Philip Kotler

Distinguished Professor of International Marketing,
Kellogg School of Management,
Northwestern University

Doing Business Globally

BACK IN 1991 I was asked by John Akers at IBM to look at the question about IBM being more customer driven. That was a very fashionable issue for many companies at the time. What John wanted, basically, was a way to know whether his various departments were thinking about the customer.

John asked me if I would go to the three-day board meeting that was coming up. I felt privileged to be able to be there as an observer, and I attended it. The first impression I had was seeing the members of the board. Remember, IBM means International Business Machines—the *I* is *International*.

I looked around, and everyone seemed to be an American. There were about thirteen people on the board, running this gigantic company. [There was] one non-American, Mr. [Kaspar] Cassani from Switzerland. I was kind of surprised. At that time, IBM was particularly profitable in Japan, and there was no sign of someone who might have been a board member from Japan.

I drew the impression that if you're going to be an international company, you really

International Companies

have to become international. We were actually no different from companies in Japan, which didn't have non-Japanese on their board. So the lesson is that you have to bring in talent from other countries—not only at the board level but also at all the levels—so that the company has multiple perspectives.

Much of my belief is that all good marketing is local. It's hard to understand the local situation if you're at corporate headquarters and you don't have some people to do that. Why don't more companies internationalize their board if they're going to be global companies? There are probably some risks. You like to be in control of the American nature of the company—that's how it's got started and where it operates, basically. But on the other hand, you're going to lose a lot by "groupthink."

One of the problems in bringing someone who is from another country on the board is the possibility that they won't feel comfortable or that they won't be ready to bring a different perspective. There might be a lot of yea-saying kind of attitudes. The important thing in carrying out such a thing is bringing some members from other countries on the board and making sure they're comfortable in speaking their views to the board, not being people who have to go along with what the majority is thinking.

TAKEAWAYS

- ⚔ For an international company to truly attain success, the company must have an international board.

- ⚔ This requires bringing in talent from across the globe at the board level, but it also helps to bring in international talent at all levels of the company.

- ⚔ Organizations often associate risk with internationalizing their boards

International Companies

because they like to be in control, but the real risk lies in the "groupthink" that occurs otherwise.

Timing Your Entry into New Markets

Lord Paul

Chairman, Caparo Group

ONE OF THE great things, in my view, that a leader must do, is look for opportunities. In business, timing is the most important thing: if you do something today it may seem to be the most wonderful time but if you do the same thing tomorrow it may be the worst time. If you just happen to be in the right place at the right time, that is most important.

Sometimes it happens by luck, at other times by keeping a constant vigil. To give yourself too much credit for your wonderful idea is just as dangerous as not making use of the opportunity.

For example, at the moment my children and I feel that India provides the best potential for manufacturing. The Chinese are very quickly becoming world leaders in manufacturing. All over the world you see Chinese products with good quality and good delivery. The only country that can compete with the Chinese is India, because in the West we are very short of workers. India has the potential for supply and demand. India has improved its education, both in quality and in quantity. It's the only country in the world that sees between three and three-and-a-half million boys and girls graduating every year.

The Chinese have shot themselves in the foot by having their birth-control one-child rule. In twenty-five years, China will be running out of young people, whereas India, because of [no limits on] birth control, will gain from that.

At the moment, all eyes are on India. But no country remains in focus all the time. Another country will come up; maybe Pakistan, maybe Sri Lanka. But we think it's India at the moment, so we go all out for it. Let's make out the project reports and so on; either we believe that it's there, or we might make a wrong decision, but [we can't] be afraid of that.

I genuinely believe that your mistakes teach you far more than your successes. The only thing you hope and pray for is that you make fewer mistakes than successes, but don't be afraid to make mistakes. We say, "Let's grab this opportunity." We are simultaneously building six plants in India at the moment because we believe then everybody else will come. If you are ahead—if you have a two-year lead in business—it's marvelous to see the results of that.

Every market has a time window. If you miss it, you will have to wait until the next opportunity comes. If you are interested in a market, keep your eyes and ears open for whenever you see it in focus, whether it's the United States, the United Kingdom, India, or China.

I'll give you an example. We went to China in 1996 to see what we could do. We found that we had already missed it by two years. I would have liked to go to China again four years ago. But then India started coming up, and we thought that since we knew India far better than China, we'd get into India. After that, ten years ago when we were in China—when we were late by two years—after six or eight years, the opportunity returned. These opportunities will come. I don't want to imply that if you don't go to India now, another opportunity will never come. It will arrive, but you will have to wait.

TAKEAWAYS

🖎 Leaders must be vigilant about market opportunities, and timing is the pivotal factor. What could be successful today might be a failure tomorrow.

🖎 Every market has a time window, so keep your eyes and ears open. Then, when you see an opportunity, don't be afraid to go after it.

🖎 If you miss an opportunity, don't give up the watch. The opportunity will likely present itself again, but you will have to wait for it.

The Opportunities and Challenges of Working in China

Michael Dell

Founder, CEO, and Chairman, Dell

Interviewer: When you think about where you're expanding and mapping a broader strategy for the operation, would China be another one of those places where it's obvious that they've been a supply chain and now they're also a market? Could you talk about the potential for China?

Michael Dell: China is our third-largest market. We've had seven years of 45 percent compounded annual growth in China. We have two factories in China. We're heading rapidly into [western China], into the tier-three, -four, -five, -six, and -seven type cities, and we're penetrating those as well.

There are uniquenesses in every market, and China has a scale that is unparalleled. We're going after it. You can find just about every principal activity of Dell occurring in China—from IT development to research and development, to manufacturing, to sales service support. You pretty much have all aspects of the company operating there.

Interviewer: How would you advise entrepreneurs who want break into that market and think about it both from, as you say, the back office or the development side as well as a consumer market?

The Opportunities and Challenges

Michael Dell: We find some differences there, but when you talk about the way larger organizations work, whether they're global companies or the large Chinese national companies, it's not dramatically different from the way large companies work in other countries. When you get into a consumer market, that could be a bit different because of credit and the scale and distribution.

And, of course, you have many different Chinas. You have the cities; you have the rural [areas]. You have all these tier-three through -seven cities. There's a multitude of opportunities. One thing we found in China is, customers really value relation-ships. So when Dell comes and we say want to have a relationship, we show up and we stay. We want to understand more about their business and more about their needs. That works. It actually works everywhere. I think it's a universal belief system that people want to have relationships.

Interviewer: Right. It is a ubiquitous princi-ple of all cultures. Certainly understanding that there are so many differences between the different Chinas is a bit like understanding the different markets that you have around the world, within the United States and Europe. Is there a description you can make of a particular visit that had impact on you when you realized that things had changed in terms of serving China?

Michael Dell: We've had to do things differently there to achieve the success. First, it's not for the faint of heart, because there are a lot of things that are changing and unpredictable. I remember at one point—this was very early on in our China experience—we'd built this brand-new factory. A bunch of guys from some government agency showed up, and they had a bunch of papers. They said we couldn't build computers from this factory anymore; it said so there on their papers. This is what we were told in the translation.

So we asked what they meant. We called over the mayor, and these guys are fighting and arguing. Two hours later, it's all solved—not a problem anymore. But that was the kind of thing that was happening quite a bit in China, just an unpredictable, almost chaotic environment where you had to ready for anything. And because it was evolving so quickly, they were making up the rules as they went along.

TAKEAWAYS

- ⚔ While uniquenesses exist in every global market, the scale of the Chinese market is unparalleled with its varied cultures and unpredictable environment.

- ⚔ Nonetheless, larger organizations in China operate in ways that are not dramatically different from other organizations.

Doing Business Globally

⚹ To succeed, be prepared to do things differently and make up the rules along the way; and most importantly, value your relationships.

Handling Adversity

Peter Birch

Former Chairman, Land Securities Group

I'M SURE THAT everybody associates Afghanistan with war, particularly in recent years. But for Gillette, Afghanistan was a major export market. In fact, a major part of a manufacturing facility in the United Kingdom was exported there.

We had an agent in Afghanistan, and we'd been doing business with him for many years. When the Russians moved into

Doing Business Globally

Afghanistan, things became a bit more difficult, but we continued to work together.

One day, we found that the agent had fallen behind in his payments by several million pounds. I was the chief executive based in the United Kingdom who was responsible for that part of the world and Europe.

One miserable, cold January, I flew out to Kabul in Afghanistan, saw the agent, Ali Yakavi, and said, "Mr. Yakavi, we've known one another for a long, long time. You owe us some $3 million. How do you propose to pay us?"

He replied, "Don't worry, you'll be paid. Come with me."

The temperature was about minus 20°— one of the coldest days I've ever imagined— in Kabul. We went up to the top floor in an old building, two floors up, and there was a man over a stove with a hood over his head because it was so cold. Ali said to me, "We'll pay your account now; we'll pay you the $3.2 million. Which bank would you like it paid on? Citibank? Bank of America? You name it."

Handling Adversity

We said Citibank because they were the bankers for Gillette. "Which city would you like it paid in? Los Angeles, Florida, Miami, or New York?" So we said Miami. This chap took his coat off, opened a drawer in his desk, took out about fifty checkbooks, found the one for CitiGroup in Miami, wrote out a check, and gave it to me. I thought, "That's going to bounce; it must bounce," because one's always cynical and skeptical.

That afternoon, I flew to Pakistan, went to the local DHL office, and sent the check off to America to be cleared. By the time I got back to London five days later, it had been cleared and we'd received the money.

The moral is that when one has difficulties, don't always assume the worst. Get off your backside, and go out and do something about it.

At that time there were Russian troops [in Afghanistan], and it was quite dangerous in Kabul. But we got our money and we continued to do business in times of adversity.

TAKEAWAYS

- ⚔ In times of war and other obstacles, global business can become more difficult, but it's nonetheless possible to continue a working relationship.

- ⚔ When times get tough or you're faced with difficult situations, don't assume the worst.

- ⚔ Instead, get out of the office and do something about it. Doing so can preserve the relationship and pave the way for continued successes.

The Art of Managing a Global Online Community

Jimmy Wales

Founder, Wikipedia, Wikimedia Foundation

BOTH WIKIPEDIA AND Wikia are fully global. Wikipedia is in more than 150 languages. Wikia is in 66 languages—we would say 67, but we don't count Klingon as a real language. We have people all over the world working on projects that are of interest to them. It's been really interesting to see how these things develop.

One of the things that's been really interesting is that people assume there's going to radical, cultural differences that are going to make it really hard to do this, when in fact most of the rules that evolve in different language communities are very similar. When the communities are left to come up with their own rules, they try things out. Some things succeed; some things fail. But they end up more or less in the same place.

And it's because a lot of the values that people have are truly universal human values. People want to be treated with respect. They want to be listened to. [If] decisions that are made that affect them personally, they want to have some say in them. They don't have to get their way all the time; they just want to participate. That's universal.

Because of that, it's been a lot easier than we would've ever imagined. We have such an open model where anyone can come and participate, and we've devised ways for people to supervise each other—little things like translating the interface of the software. It just takes one person to do it. If they do a bad job of it, somebody else can complain and go in and fix it. So we've been able to overcome the language barrier in that way. People just do whatever they want in their own language.

We were very concerned in the early days of Wikipedia about what would happen in the small-language Wikipedias, where we didn't have anyone who could go out and supervise what they're doing. What are they going to do? Are they going to make a proper Wikipedia, or is it going to be a radical political site?

Somebody brought me an example once. They said they had a real problem. There was a concern that in the Tatar-language Wikipedia: there was a statement on the front page that said, "Long live the Tatars." It had been there for more than a year. I didn't think that sounded good. It sounded nationalistic or something. I wasn't really sure what was going on there. But it was like saying "God save the Queen" or "God bless America" on the front page of the English-language Wikipedia.

But we wanted to be very respectful of the community. We didn't want to just go in, delete it and tell them to knock it off. They might get [rebellious]; we just didn't know what might happen—some of the lessons I had learned from other communities. So we gently reached out to them. We found someone who spoke the local language. We enquired about what was up, and their answer was, "We never really thought about. Okay, we'll take it down." It was further explained that it was a sentiment like, "God save the Queen." It was just something they said. It didn't have a lot of deep political meaning. It wasn't a statement of Tatar independence or anything like that; it was just something they did. That was a case where we thought there was a problem, but it turned out it was really not a big problem.

The key learning in that particular case was that we could trust these communities—that if you get together eight to ten people from anywhere on the planet, in any language, and they're operating in a peer-to-peer way, you'll get enough checks and balances naturally. Things may be not quite the way you would want them, but they're going to be pretty close.

We went to them and treated them with respect. We didn't come in and say, top-down, "We don't allow nationalist state-ments on the front page. You have to take that down." Instead we just said, "Hey, can you explain this to us?" Then they real-ized and understood immediately that they should take down the statement.

It was that kind of respect for the com-munity and the assumption of good faith that was something that I was really pleased with and a little bit surprised by. I was very nervous that we were going to have a Tatar Wikipedia spin-off or something. But it turned out to be no problem.

———•••———

TAKEAWAYS

———•••———

⚑ When working on a global level, there's a tendency for people to assume that cultural differences will make it hard for organizations to work together.

⚑ In reality, most of the rules and values that evolve in different language communities are similar. All people want is to be listened to and treated with respect.

⚑ When problems surface, approaching the issue from a position of respect and good faith often turns the problem into a nonissue.

━━━ ◆◆◆ ━━━

Maintain Ethics in Difficult Conditions

Sir Paul Judge

Deputy Chairman, Royal Society of Arts

━━━ ◆◆◆ ━━━

DURING THE 1970S I was at Cadbury Schweppes as a financial analyst and then deputy finance director. In the early 1980s, I was asked to go to Kenya as managing director, which was my first real executive position, four thousand miles from the head office. And, of course, it was quite different from working in London or my previous experience doing my MBA in the United States. So there was a lot of adjustment to local conditions. There were obviously things to do with the company itself but also to do with the wider environment.

The thing that impacted most was the government, and we had a lot of issues with regulation. The particular issues we had were with the government and price control. They had a devastating effect on the business. The operations covered both confectionery and food on one side, but also soft drinks. We were the Pepsi bottler, the 7-Up bottler, and, of course, the Schweppes bottler.

The confectionery and foods side worked very well, and there was no price control, because that was seen as being sold largely to the European and more affluent part of the country. But the soft drinks were a basic good; indeed, in many countries it is one of the very first consumer goods that people purchase as the affluence level grows. And so it was heavily price controlled.

Maintain Ethics in Difficult Conditions

But sadly, it wasn't just price controlled; there was also a sales tax on it of 50 percent. We, as a Western company, were competing against a number of franchisees of other brands—and they didn't really have as clear an ethical position as we had. Therefore, they tended to underdeclare their sales and, as a result, they collected the sales tax, but they didn't pay over the whole of it to the government. So they made an immediate profit with sales tax at 50 percent without having to worry too much about the price of soft drinks.

So when we would be lobbying the government for a price increase, the other bottlers would not really be worried about that. The consequence of that was that eventually we had to arrange to sell off two of our bottling plants to local people who could then manage it in the way that they thought right. But clearly Cadbury Schweppes, as an ethical Western company, couldn't indulge in those sorts of practices. The only solution, sadly, was to sell off the two plants.

Doing Business Globally

The experience taught me that governments can be quite difficult, and regulation is very important. It also taught me the rule of law is key, because you have to have a level playing field in competitive activities, and that if a government doesn't allow a level playing field, then in fact there will inevitably be difficulties for those who try and uphold the higher standards.

When you go to a new country, you have to adjust and have to understand, and it's no good trying to take all of the practices and procedures from one country to another. But you do have to have a core of ethics that you take with you and there are certain standards that you are not going to change, even if there are extreme pressures. You have to find other commercial solutions that keep the company ethical but nevertheless try and gain the commercial advantages you're looking for.

TAKEAWAYS

- When working in new locations, be prepared to adjust not only to local conditions but also to the wider environment.

- Governments can be difficult, and regulation is extremely important. If the government doesn't allow a level playing field, you'll encounter great difficulties.

- When faced with extreme pressures, seek commercial advantages that don't compromise your core ethics, even if it means getting out of the market.

Developing Global Citizens

Blythe McGarvie

President and Founder,
Leadership for International Finance

THIS LESSON IS really about how important it is to be a global citizen and also how you cannot come into a situation with preconceived ideas.

When I was working at Sara Lee, there was a man named Phil. Phil used to work for Sears during its heyday, its successful days, and he had joined Hanes Hosiery years ago and was head of our Hanes Hosiery business, living a comfortable life in Winston-Salem, North Carolina.

He was about sixty years old, and my boss asked him if he would go run our Australian business in the Pacific Rim. Australia? Fifteen thousand miles away? Australia is called the land of Oz for more reasons than just because Aussie is a nickname for Oz. Oz is a strange place. Business is done differently; the language is even a little different. It's not an easy place to adjust to, and you're far away from home. But Phil said yes.

Phil's kids were pretty much grown, and his wife, Elaine, was [adventuresome]. He turned out to be one of the best presidents we ever had in Australia. He would call me every Friday night, after I came home from work; it was Saturday morning his time, and he'd review the week with me. He'd talk about what he'd learned, what he had done, some of the risks. He would say, "I never worked so hard. Here in Australia, I don't have the support systems at headquarters. I don't have the support that I used to have. This is tough work."

Developing Global Citizens

But I learned that he was excited about his job. He loved what he was doing. He was exploring new worlds. He was growing, even at age sixty. The lesson I learned from this is, just because somebody might be getting into traditional twilight of their career, don't assume that person won't take on new adventures and new risks. Turns out, he was the best employee because he knew how to handle customers; he knew how to lead a team; he even knew how to develop a successor.

I learned so much from him on those Friday night calls. My husband used to say "Why are you taking these calls at night? You've had a long week already." But they were so meaningful, and we'd established a relationship. I haven't worked for Phil in fifteen years, but we still stay in touch once or twice a year. And he really helped me, because when I moved to France for my job, I always kept in mind some of the advice that he gave me.

One piece of advice was, when you move away—you have to keep in touch. You have to reach out to headquarters, because they don't think about you. You're out in the

Doing Business Globally

distant world. A true global citizen knows that you're the one out being the pioneer, and the only way to garner support is to do your job really well in that new country but also to recognize that you have to link in the people from the home country, so they understand what's going on. That's a true global citizen and, also, it changes everyone's perceptions. You learn, and you help people at home learn as well.

To be successful, you have to adapt and adopt. By that, I mean you have to adapt to a new environment, learn how the new country or the new people are doing things. That's so important. You have to come to them on their terms, and then sometimes you have to adopt new customs.

For example, one of the things that had never been done before, is Phil never used to call people on Friday nights/Saturday mornings to fill them in on what was going on, but he was developing me. He was developing leaders. He'd learned to adapt to a whole new style of working, yet he was still developing and always believed:

Developing Global Citizens

Today, the time I spend may not benefit my business right now, but I'm developing a future leader.

I really thank Phil for helping me become a global citizen. He was critical in teaching me what it takes, and developing others is so satisfying. I try and do it myself. That is a mark of a true leader—someone who says, "Let me develop someone."

We weren't all born experts at age sixteen, as a great CEO. You have to learn, you have to watch, and you have to pay attention, but it also helps if someone out there helps you develop.

TAKEAWAYS

⊰ When working abroad, leave any preconceived notions behind and be prepared to develop a support system with your home office.

Doing Business Globally

🪶 Those who move away are challenged not only with adapting to and adopting a new environment, but also by doing their job really well and reaching out to headquarters.

🪶 To be a true global citizen, you need to recognize that you're the pioneer and that it's your job to change perceptions both at home and abroad.

⇥ ABOUT THE ⇤
CONTRIBUTORS

Sir David Bell is a Director of Pearson, an international media company. He is also Chairman of the Financial Times Group, having been Chief Executive of the Financial Times since 1993.

In July 1998 Sir David was appointed Pearson's Director for People with responsibility for the recruitment, motivation, development, and reward of employees across the Pearson Group. In addition, he is a Director of *The Economist*; the Vitec Group, Plc; and The Windmill Partnership. Sir David is Chairman of Common Purpose International, Chairman of Crisis, Chairman of Sadler's Wells, and Chairman of the International Youth Foundation.

He was also Chairman of the Millennium Bridge Trust (1995–2002), responsible for conceiving the first new bridge across the Thames in the center of London in one hundred years.

Sir David was educated at Cambridge University and the University of Pennsylvania.

Peter Birch is the former Chairman of Land Securities Group, the United Kingdom's largest real estate investment trust.

About the Contributors

From 1958 to 1965, Mr. Birch worked for Nestlé in the United Kingdom, Switzerland, Singapore, and Malaysia.

He held various positions between 1965 and 1984 with Gillette Industries, the consumer products group. This included time as Managing Director of Gillette UK, Ltd. and Group General Manager for Africa, Middle East, and Eastern Europe.

His next fourteen years were spent as Chief Executive of Abbey National, during which time he oversaw the successful transition of the building society into a bank. He left the company in 1998.

From 1998 to 2006, Mr. Birch served as Chairman of Land Securities, the provider of commercial accommodation and property services.

He is currently a Director of Trinity Mirror, a position he has held since 1999. He was Chairman from 1998 to 1999. He is also Chairman of Kensington Group and Director of Travelex Group.

Michael Dell is the founder, CEO, and Chairman of Dell, Inc., the direct-sales computer company he founded in 1984. He is also the author of *Direct from Dell: Strategies That Revolutionized an Industry*.

Mr. Dell started his computer company with $1,000 and a goal to build relationships directly with customers. By 1992 he had become the youngest CEO to earn a place among the *Fortune* 500. In 1998 he formed MSD Capital, a private investment firm. In 2001 Dell ranked number-one in global market share.

About the Contributors

Mr. Dell serves on the Foundation Board of the World Economic Forum and the executive committee of its International Business Council. He is a member of the U.S. Business Council. Mr. Dell also serves on the U.S. President's Council of Advisors on Science and Technology and the Governing Board of the Indian School of Business in Hyderabad, India.

E. Neville Isdell is Chairman of the Board and Chief Executive Officer of the Coca-Cola Company.

In 1966 Mr. Isdell joined the Coca-Cola Company at a local bottling company in Zambia. From then until 1989, he held a variety of positions and was Senior Vice President of the company from January 1989 to February 1998. He also served as President of the Greater Europe Group from January 1995 to February 1998.

Mr. Isdell was also Chairman and Chief Executive Officer of Coca-Cola Beverages Plc, from July 1998 to September 2000. He was Chief Executive Officer of Coca-Cola Hellenic Bottling Company S.A. from September 2000 to May 2001 and Vice Chairman from May 2001 to December 2001. From January 2002 to May 2004, Mr. Isdell was an international consultant to the company.

Mr. Isdell has been Chairman and CEO of the highly recognizable Coca-Cola Company since June 2004. He is also a Director of SunTrust Banks, Inc., a position he has held since December 2004.

About the Contributors

Sir Paul Judge is the Deputy Chair of the Royal Society of Arts (RSA), an organization dedicated to removing barriers to social progress.

After graduating from Trinity College, Cambridge, and earning an MBA at the Wharton Business School, Sir Paul subsequently spent thirteen years with Cadbury Schweppes Plc. He then led the buyout of their food companies to form Premier Brands, which was successfully sold in 1989.

He went on to become a government-appointed Member of the Milk Marketing Board, Chairman of Food from Britain, Director General of the Conservative Party, a Ministerial Adviser at the U.K. Cabinet Office, a Director of the Boddington Group, and a Director of WPP. In addition he was the key benefactor of the Judge Institute of Management at the University of Cambridge.

Sir Paul is currently Chairman of the British North American Committee and President of the Association of MBAs. He is also a Director of Tempur-Pedic International.

Rosabeth Moss Kanter is a renowned Harvard Business School professor (holding the Ernest L. Arbuckle Chair) and bestselling author whose strategic and practical insights have guided leaders of large and small organizations for more than twenty-five years.

She is the former editor of *Harvard Business Review* (1989–1992) and a consultant to major corporations and governments worldwide on issues of strategy, innovation, and leadership for change. She has been named to lists of the "50 most powerful women in the world" (*Times* of London), placed in the top 10 on the annual list of the "50 most influential business thinkers in the world" (Accenture and Thinkers 50), and called one of the nine "rock stars of business" (American Way).

Kanter is the author or coauthor of seventeen books, which have been translated into seventeen languages. Her classic prizewinning book *Men and Women of the Corporation* was a source of insight to countless individuals and organizations about corporate careers and the individual and organizational factors that can load the situation for success; a spin-off cartoon video, *A Tale of "O": On Being Different*, is among the world's most widely used diversity tools; and a related book, *Work and Family in the United States*, set a policy agenda (in 2001 a coalition of centers created the Rosabeth Moss Kanter Award for the best research on that issue).

Her award-winning book *When Giants Learn to Dance* showed many companies worldwide the way to master the new terms of competition at the dawn of the global information age. Her latest book is *America the Principled: 6 Opportunities for Becoming a Can-Do Nation Once Again*.

Philip Kotler is the S.C. Johnson & Son Professor of International Marketing at the Kellogg School of Management, Northwestern University.

Professor Kotler is the author of several books,

About the Contributors

including *Marketing Management: Analysis, Planning, Implementation and Control*, the most widely used marketing book in graduate business schools worldwide. He has published more than one hundred articles in leading journals, several of which have received best-article awards.

Professor Kotler has consulted for such companies as IBM Corporation; General Electric Company; AT&T Corporation; Honeywell International, Inc.; Bank of America Corporation; Merck & Co., Inc.; and others in the areas of marketing strategy and planning, marketing organization, and international marketing.

He has been Chairman of the College of Marketing of the Institute of Management Sciences, a Director of the American Marketing Association, a Trustee of the Marketing Science Institute, a Director of the MAC Group, a former member of the Yankelovich Advisory Board, and a member of the Copernicus Advisory Board. He is a member of the Board of Governors of the School of the Art Institute of Chicago and a member of the Advisory Board of the Drucker Foundation.

Maurice Lévy is the Chairman and CEO of Publicis Groupe.

Mr. Lévy joined Publicis, one of the world's largest advertising and media services conglomerates, in 1971. He was given responsibility for its data processing and information technology systems.

However, he moved swiftly up the organization,

being appointed Corporate Secretary in 1973, Managing Director in 1976, and Chairman and CEO of Publicis Conseil in 1981.

He then became Vice Chair of Publicis Groupe in 1986, and Vice Chair of the Management Board in 1988. He was appointed Chairman and CEO of the Management Board in November 1987.

Mr. Lévy sits on the Board of the World Economic Foundation.

Blythe McGarvie is the President and Founder of Leadership for International Finance.

Ms. McGarvie has operated profitable business units and managed employees in business endeavors from China to France and Finland. Prior to starting the Leadership for International Finance, Ms. McGarvie served as Executive Vice President and CFO for BIC Group from 1999 to 2002.

She is the author of *Fit In, Stand Out: Mastering the FISO Factor: The Key to Leadership Effectiveness in Business and Life*.

Since 2003, Ms. McGarvie has been President and Founder of Leadership for International Finance, a private consulting firm offering a global perspective for clients to achieve profitable growth, and providing leadership seminars for corporate and academic groups. She has extensive knowledge of consumer markets, the worldwide economy, and the development of financial literacy.

She has served on the Boards of Accenture since 2001, Pepsi Bottling Group since 2002, St. Paul Travelers since 2003, and Viacom since 2007.

About the Contributors

Ms. McGarvie was recently appointed Senior Fellow for Northwestern University's Kellogg Innovation Network.

Lord Paul is Chairman of Caparo Group, a leading manufacturer of steel, automotive, and general engineering products.

Lord Paul earned his MSc in Mechanical Engineering at the Massachusetts Institute of Technology. In 1968, he founded the Caparo Group with one small factory in Huntingdon, in the United Kingdom.

He has been a Labor peer since 1996, and has served as a member of a number of Parliamentary Select Committees. He is currently a co-opted member of the European Union Sub-committee addressing the Internal Market.

Lord Paul is the British Ambassador for Overseas Business. He is also a member of the U.K. Department of Trade and Industry's Indo-British Partnership, advising on steel, mining, and investment interests.

Lord Paul was President of the U.K. Steel Association in 1994 and 1995, and has been the Chancellor of the University of Wolverhampton since 1998. He was named the first Chancellor of the University of Westminster in March 2006.

Sir Bob Reid is the Chairman of ICE Clear Europe and the Former Deputy Governor of Halifax Bank of Scotland.

About the Contributors

Sir Bob joined Shell International Petroleum Company Limited in 1956 and spent much of his career overseas, including posts in Brunei, Nigeria, Thailand, and Australia.

He was Chairman and Chief Executive of Shell UK from 1985 until September 1990. He was Chairman of the British Railways Board from 1990 until he retired in 1995. Sir Bob was Deputy Governor of Halifax Bank of Scotland from 1997 to 2004. He then served as Chairman of Avis Europe from May 2002 until he retired from the Board in May 2004.

In 2007, Sir Bob became Chairman of ICE's wholly owned European clearinghouse ICE Clear Europe. He has been Director of ICE since June 2001 and has served as Chairman of the International Petroleum Exchange (today known as ICE Futures) since 1999.

Sir Bob has been Lead Director of CHC Helicopter Corporation since 2005, after joining the Board in 2004. He is also Director of Diligenta Limited and Merchants Trust plc.

Bryan Sanderson is the Former Chairman of Standard Chartered. He is currently Chairman of urban regeneration company Sunderland arc and Co-chairman of the British Government's Asia Task Force.

Mr. Sanderson spent thirty-six years at BP in positions that included Managing Director and Chief Executive of BP Nutrition in 1987, Chief

Executive of BP Chemicals three years later, and then a main Board Director.

In 1992 he was appointed a Managing Director of BP, with group responsibility for Asia Pacific. He continued as CEO of BP Chemicals until 2000.

Mr. Sanderson served as Chairman of Standard Chartered Bank, Plc. from 2003 to 2006. His focus on governance issues strengthened the Board and contributed to the Bank's continued growth in shareholder value and market capitalization.

Mr. Sanderson is also Co-chairman with the Secretary of State for Trade and Industry of the Asia Task Force, created by the British government in 2004 to examine means of lowering barriers to trade between the United Kingdom and Asia.

Andrew Sherman is the cofounder and CEO of Grow Fast Grow Right, a world leader in the development and delivery of on-site and online executive and management training programs.

Mr. Sherman, a recognized corporate and transactional attorney, is also a partner in the Washington, D.C.–based law firm Dickstein Shapiro. He serves as a legal and strategic adviser to *Fortune* 500 and emerging growth companies.

Mr. Sherman has also served as an adjunct professor in the MBA programs at the University of Maryland for more than eighteen years. Since 1987 he has been outside general counsel to the Young Entrepreneurs' Organization, and he is Chairman of the Board/General Counsel to the Small and

Emerging Contractors Advisory Forum. He is the former Chairman of the National Commission on Entrepreneurship.

Jimmy Wales is the founder of Wikipedia, the free open-content encyclopedia.

From 1994 to 2000 Mr. Wales was the Research Director at Chicago Options Associates, a futures and options trading firm in Chicago. In 2000 he started the open-content encyclopedia Nupedia. In 2001 he founded Wikipedia, a free, online encyclopedia that anyone can edit.

Mr. Wales is the Chairman of Wikimedia Foundation Inc., a nonprofit charitable organization dedicated to encouraging the growth, development, and distribution of free, multilingual content. He is the Cofounder of Wiki, Inc., a wiki farm that includes collection of wikis on different topics, all hosted on the same site.

He is a Fellow at the Berkman Center for Internet & Society at Harvard Law School and a Director of Socialtext, a leading provider of Enterprise 2.0 solutions. He is also Director of Creative Commons, a nonprofit licensing organization.

In 2006 Mr. Wales was named as one of *Time* magazine's people who shape our world, and in 2007 he was named as a *Forbes* magazine Web celebrity.

⊰ ACKNOWLEDGMENTS ⊱

First and foremost, a heartfelt thanks goes to all of the executives who have candidly shared their hard-earned experience and battle-tested insights for the Lessons Learned series.

Angelia Herrin at Harvard Business School Publishing consistently offered unwavering support, good humor, and counsel from the inception of this ambitious project.

Brian Surette, Hollis Heimbouch, and David Goehring provided invaluable editorial direction, perspective, and encouragement. Much appreciation goes to Jennifer Lynn for her research and diligent attention to detail. Many thanks to the entire HBSP team of designers, copy editors, and marketing professionals who helped bring this series to life.

Finally, thanks to our fellow cofounder James MacKinnon and the entire Fifty

Acknowledgments

Lessons team for the tremendous amount of time, effort, and steadfast support for this project.

—Adam Sodowick
   Andy Hasoon
   Directors and Cofounders
   Fifty Lessons